LONDON

Edited by Claire Tupholme

First published in Great Britain in 2003 by
YOUNG WRITERS
Remus House,
Coltsfoot Drive,
Peterborough, PE2 9JX
Telephone (01733) 890066

HB ISBN 0 75434 219 0
SB ISBN 0 75434 220 4

FOREWORD

This year, the Young Writers' The Write Stuff! competition proudly presents a showcase of the best poetic talent from over 40,000 up-and-coming writers nationwide.

Young Writers was established in 1991 and we are still successful, even in today's modern world, in promoting and encouraging the reading and writing of poetry.

The thought, effort, imagination and hard work put into each poem impressed us all, and once again, the task of selecting poems was a difficult one, but nevertheless, an enjoyable experience.

We hope you are as pleased as we are with the final selection and that you and your family continue to be entertained with *The Write Stuff! London* for many years to come.

CONTENTS

JFS School, Kenton

The Poems

AUTUMN

Rain drizzling down
Falling like a drop of snow,
Autumn starts again.

Daylight trickles out of the skyline
like water through a sieve,
Evening is here, stars shine so brightly,
very dark sky spreading through the night.
In comes the moon, arriving so gracefully,
no more leaves falling down,
nor the yellow or brown.
Autumn ends and winter starts,
dull and snowy through the night.

Cars skidding, snowdrops,
Spitting drops fall on the ground,
Winter is ending.

Devina Morjaria (10)

SWIMMING

Splash goes the water
Flash go the waves
Clash go the children
And bash goes the swimming apparatus.

Chisom A Diogu (9)

SPOILT BRAT

I hate my mum
I hate my dad
When I'm really, really mad.
It doesn't matter how hard they try
If I don't get what I want to buy
I cry all night
I cry all day
Until I get my own way.
Everyone says that I'm a spoilt little brat,
But I don't care because they're just jealous little prats.

Su Firat (13)
Elizabeth Garrett Anderson Girls' School, Islington

SEASONS

Summer -
Summer is hot and when I get a tan,
Summer is when people go on holiday,
Summer is when people go on picnics.
Summer is when everywhere is shining with brightness,
Summer is a season when people are smiling,
Summer is a season when everyone tries to have nice feelings.
Summer, summer, summer.

Winter -
Winter is when we are all shivering,
Winter is when we all run outside to make snowmen.
Winter is when we open our radiators,
Winter is when we have Christmas.
Winter is when it gets dark so early,
Winter is when it is so cold,
Winter is when we all have nice feelings for each other.

Spring -
Spring is when we actually don't know how the weather is going to be,
Spring is when we think it's going to be chilly.
Spring is when our thoughts are weird.
Spring is when it's dark when we wake up.
Spring is when we are lazy going to school or work.

Autumn -
Autumn is when it's warm in the day and cold at night,
Autumn is when the leaves start falling.
Autumn is when we don't like getting homework.

Mehtap Ornek (13)
Elizabeth Garrett Anderson Girls' School, Islington

IN MEMORY OF JOHNNY

I feel down, I feel blue,
I feel unhappy and so should you.
'Cause a little boy Johnny did disappear
and they found his body after a year.
He was my brother, and that is true,
He loved me lots and I loved him too.
We used to play games, always be fair,
Except when he went over the top and
started to pull my hair.
It is time for this to end -
I was lying all along, but I had to pretend.

Jadene Lucia Nemorin (13)
Elizabeth Garrett Anderson Girls' School, Islington

I HATE YOU!

I hate the way you look at me
I hate the way you talk to me
I hate it when you hold me close
I hate it when you whisper gently
I hate it when you touch me
I hate your water-blue eyes
I hate your silky hair
I hate it when you kiss me

But what I hate most, is the way
I love you.

Olivia Butler (13)
Elizabeth Garrett Anderson Girls' School, Islington

THE WORD I FEARED

This may seem weird
But there's something I feared,

From the day I was born,
To the end of dawn.

This fear is locked inside me,
And I don't know what it might be.

This fear, I don't know,
Is stuck inside me, like a bow.

The word that flutters past my eyes,
Is something that I see in the skies.

Now that I know what the word may be,
Please may the word be deceived from me.

Algerta Stafa (13)
Elizabeth Garrett Anderson Girls' School, Islington

ANTS

I'm a little ant crawling down the street
Oh, there's a piece of sandwich
Shall I go, shall I not?
Shall I go, shall I not?
I'll go and have a bite.
Oh no, here they come - giants!
Run away, run away
But no, they don't forgive me.

Squash! The first foot treads on me,
I'm nearly dead.
Please forgive me.
Squash! The second foot,
Ha, ha, ha!
They start giggling, how funny.
Finally they go, but I'm squashed,
What's the point? I think.
I don't hurt you, you don't hurt me,
But no, I finally die.

Rahime Bilgic (13)
Elizabeth Garrett Anderson Girls' School, Islington

COMPETITION

Friends are the best
Friends are like a diary
They keep your secrets
If you promise them, not to tell
Friends are everything
They stick by your side
Even if you're down.

My friends are there when you need them
They're nice to be around
They're there when you're down
They like to take you out to see
Whatever is on at the movies.
They also talk to you about whatever is
On their minds
They trust you to tell.
I feel I can trust them because
They're always there for me.

Juliet Tordecilla (13)
Elizabeth Garrett Anderson Girls' School, Islington

MY FRIEND AND HER CAT

My friend's just a small little girl,
With long, blonde, curly curls.
She also wears a lot of pearls
And likes doing lots of twirls.
She has a pretty little kitty,
That she calls Nicky,
Who's always licky, licky, licking.

Stacey Erdogan (13)
Elizabeth Garrett Anderson Girls' School, Islington

SEASON TIME

Imagine a dead summer
Without berries or buds in sight
The leaves of the willow
Are dead on my pillow
Every day, pouring wet
The power of the sun
Is still not born.
Water, water - pouring down
I wish I could reverse it back
Mirror, mirror on the wall
Bring summer back to us all.

Samaa El-Nasser (13)
Elizabeth Garrett Anderson Girls' School, Islington

MY MUMMY SAYS . . .

My mummy told me never to take drugs
Because they are for thugs
You get high -
I'd rather eat pie.

Stephanie Abrahams (14)
Elizabeth Garrett Anderson Girls' School, Islington

INNOCENCE

Society creates my bad habits, shortcomings
Feeding the greed of others
It wants me to become accustomed
To its rut
Yet, I do not believe all I hear, all I see,
I only believe what I feel.
Within the depths of my logic sits
A perfect plan.
A need to disperse this bubbling theory
The common sense of peace
They'll *'Ooo'* and *'Aaahh'* in wonder
Or in recollection of a long-lost memory
I name this memory *Innocence*
Innocence, ominous, virtue
All-seeing, all-knowing.

Robina Lamche-Brennan (15)
Hampstead School, Cricklewood

A Memory Of The Beach

It can be held in the very palm of your hands
It feels smooth, ragged, heavy and light all at the same time
The colours differ, depending on your taste
It is a magnificent work of natural art, that has shaped its way
through many years of drifting.
Every drift is a result of a fabulous body.
It is either waiting for you or hiding, waiting to be discovered.
For people who find it's just an object, probably won't find its secret.
A secret in some way but more a well preserved message.
A gentle placing to the ear and there the message is unfolded.
No dialling needed, no pay as you go and no quarterly bills,
just a quick free link to the sea.
A memory of the sea for any time and anywhere,
for years to go on . . .

Vincent Marsden (14)
Hampstead School, Cricklewood

BUT I DIDN'T

I cried that night,
Everybody had someone
But I didn't.
They had someone to look to
But I didn't.
The people around me, they laughed
But I didn't.
The force, they had each other
But I didn't.
The suffering of the people,
People crying, crying for family.
Crying for friends.
The war should stop
I cried that night
But my brother didn't.

Angela Mills (14)
Hampstead School, Cricklewood

RUN AWAY!

Vicious cries of hate fill the air
on the journey home,
The taste of sweat haunts my mouth
as I run from the culprits,
The speeding blur of hurled rocks fly just past my head,
The feel of the strong wind makes it increasingly
harder to run.
And the smell of hard earth gets more distinctive as
I come crashing down to it . . .

Niall Ewan Trace (13)
Hampstead School, Cricklewood

STOP THE ROT

Stop.
Stop the Devil blessing your every word,
Stop all of the anger you seem to have heard.
Stop trying to hold the Devil's tongue,
You know your neck is itching to speak,
We know that evil is ready to peak.

Why do you always seem to throw abuse
And always seem to refuse
When people tell you to stop
You carry on hurting the lot.
The evilness that is outside, keeps
On popping out for you to try. Please
Don't do it, it is wrong.
Stop. Stop now.
The killing is much too strong.

Now I am going to lash you with my fearful tongue
And you will learn right from wrong.
What can I say? The hurting has been done,
This racist woman just keeps hurting everyone.
Her malicious tongue
Keeps lashing like Hell
Trying to break loose.

But I tie it into a knot
And it slips
Back down her throat.
She trips
Because one day she will know she has lost
And will be left to count the cost.
Stop. Stop. Stop the rot.

Kara Black (13)
Highbury Fields School For Girls, Islington

STONE COLD

Frostbite giving me cold feet,
My stomach growls, aching for food.
The wind rushes past me, biting my skin
While I wait in a doorway, nowhere to go.
So thirsty. My mouth is as dry as the desert,
I feel so worthless and filthy.
Trying to curl up on the stone, cold ground.
I worry about what the next day will bring.
The cuts on my hands sting from the icy wind,
I'm so lonely, it's like there's no one else here.
I'm an invisible spirit wandering the streets,
Waiting to see if I will be moved on.
Or be left hungry, wet and depressed for the night.

Sabah Adams (13)
Highbury Fields School For Girls, Islington

LITTLE RED RIDING HOOD - THE REAL STORY

'What big teeth you have,' the wolf replied,
Claws itching and looking so snide.
'All the better to eat you with,' snapped wolf, with eyes gleaming
And with that, the child was screaming
Her body shaking and eyes streaming.

She ran and ran as fast as the wind
But cunning old wolf just sat there and grinned
Because he'd bolted the door
When Little Red Riding Hood had fallen on the floor.
Now there was no way to escape
Nothing to save her, not even her cape.
She was a goner, this girl like a doll,
As wolf gulped, he swallowed her whole.
Now the deed was done and through
The wolf's wildest dreams had all come true.

But not for long, may I add
For someone was knocking on the door like mad.
'Alright, alright!' cried the happy killer
And in came the woodcutter who lived in the villa.
He politely asked, 'What was all that noise about?'
But before he could answer, from his belly came a shout.
'And what was that?' asked the woodcutter, tall and stout.
While wolf gulped and stammered as his tummy said, 'Let us out!'

So the angry woodcutter, axe in his clutch
Chopped open wolf's stomach, and was shocked so much,
For out came granny and Red Riding Hood
And they lived their lives, happy and good.
But as for wolf, who wasn't so brave,
He lived out his life, buried in a grave.

Lauren Hounsell (12)
Highbury Fields School For Girls, Islington

AUTUMN DAYS

It was a gloomy day
And the clouds were grey
The golden leaves were falling
From the branchy trees.

Red, brown and orange leaves
Floating quietly down
To the ground
And staying there all day
Until the wind blows them away.

The trees were sad and cold
Although they looked big and bold
The leaves didn't seem to care
And left the trees all bare.

It was a gloomy day
And the clouds were grey
The golden leaves were falling
From the branchy trees.

When the leaves
Came slowly down to Earth.
They lay carelessly on the turf
Even when it rains
They lie thoughtlessly on the windowpanes.

It was a gloomy day
And the clouds were grey
The golden leaves were falling
From the branchy trees.

Ely Nunes (13)
Holland Park School, Kensington & Chelsea

AUTUMN

Now that it's autumn,
The trees aren't so very awesome.
They all look old
And some are getting bold,
Some are changing colour
And when I went to visit it with my mother
The leaves were turning yellow and brown,
Well that's what I saw.
And as the days go past
I don't really think they'll last.
It's the third season in the year,
So you will have to change your gear.
Now that the days are getting really cold,
This poem's going to have to fold.

Abbas Ghahremani (13)
Holland Park School, Kensington & Chelsea

AUTUMN GLOOM

Autumn's not my best season,
I don't find it a lot of fun.
Brown leaves falling everywhere,
I'd prefer the summer sun.

Everything's dull in autumn
Trees brown, blue skies now grey.
I'd much prefer a fresh and fragrant,
Zesty, new spring day.

The weather won't make its mind up,
If it's chilly or if it's nice.
I'd much prefer winter when,
Every day's as cold as ice.

Autumn's not my best season,
But it'll all be over soon.
Then another whole year to wait
Before the autumn gloom.

Lizzie Cross (13)
Holland Park School, Kensington & Chelsea

DEAD SOLDIER

Show respect to the dead soldier
Who fought for his rights and his life,
Be the one to show respect
As the dead soldier is now in Heaven,
Close your eyes and show respect to
The dead soldier.

He went through Hell before reaching Heaven
For his people and his country.
But no one showed respect to
The dead soldier.

No one had won, all was lost,
After all that effort and all that fighting,
Come to his funeral and show respect to
The dead soldier.

All was gone and all was lost
But still no one showed respect to
The dead soldier!

Rami Saffiedeen (13)
Holland Park School, Kensington & Chelsea

AUTUMN

The sunshine's gone
Autumn is here
Hallowe'en and bonfires
Will soon be near.

Leaves turning
Red and brown
Slowly falling
To the ground.

The rain making
Puddles on the floor.
Making autumn
A real big bore.

The sky slowly
Turning grey.
Farmers taking
In bundles of hay.

Children ready to
Trick or treat
Long gone has
The summer heat.

Danielle Carter (14)
Holland Park School, Kensington & Chelsea

AUTUMN'S TALE

Summer goes, autumn comes
The sun's out, the rain is in.
The trees die, the leaves crash down
Hallowe'en comes, holidays out.

In Hallowe'en, the monsters come
Children scare, adults shake.
Children get sweets, adults waste money,
Hallowe'en is best about autumn.

Bonfire Night, Guy Fawkes returns
Fireworks go off,
Guy Fawkes goes with a big bang
Houses of Parliament come crashing down.

The trees are tall and old
The leaves go brown and dull.
The fruits go nasty and horrible
All at once, everything comes crashing down.

Summer ends, autumn's in
The sun is gone and the rain comes in.
Do you like autumn? I say no.
The reason why, you never know whether it's hot or cold.

Leaves are brown, orange and yellow
It doesn't matter what colour it is.
They come tumbling down at once,
The reason why is because autumn's here

Nicholas Asamoah (13)
Holland Park School, Kensington & Chelsea

AUTUMN

Autumn is cold
The leaves become gold
So wrap yourselves up into warm comfy clothes.
Don't get the flu
Or your face will go blue
So take care of yourselves
When going outdoors.

Hallowe'en is coming
So dress yourselves up.
Go to doors tap, tap!
'Trick or treat, trick or treat, give us some sweets'
And go yum, yum, yum!

Bonfire nights are coming
All the colourful fireworks will be zooming
Wear hats and gloves or your hands will be gone
So try and be safe,
Very, very safe!

So enjoy autumn
As much as you can
And say woosh, boosh, yum, yum, yum!

Ruji Ambia Khanum (13)
Holland Park School, Kensington & Chelsea

MONSTERS

Sometimes in the middle of the night,
You may wake up with a scare.
Watch your back
'Cause your room may be black.
Check under your bed and in your closet,
Because something may pop out, eg a black object.
Tap, tap, tap from your window, try to scream
But the monsters have covered up your mouth.
When day breaks and you go down to breakfast,
Your mother will ask, 'What was all that noise last night?'
You will reply - 'It was the monsters!'

Oscar John West (11)
Holland Park School, Kensington & Chelsea

FAVOURITE THINGS I LIKE...
I KNOW MY FANTASY ISLAND

All the birds singing and the sky moving.
Wonderful, I think!
Nothing can go wrong - can it?
Things change in this world, I am starting to get scared.
A dark cloud is coming and the birds' singing has turned to a silent hall.
Shaking like a jelly, I ran away.
You were right, I shouldn't have come here.

I don't know where I am now,
So I am sitting beside a tree, frightened, calling for help.
Lost in this world is not a good thing.
At last, help came
Nothing will get me back into that world, nothing.
Don't go there, I'm warning you!

Quy Van Vo (12)
Holland Park School, Kensington & Chelsea

THE ALLEYWAY

As I walk through the alleyway,
It was night not day.
Something skids past me
But it couldn't be.
An image comes right at me,
I'm going blind,
I can't see
I'm walking in the graveyard,
Ouch!
Something bashed my knee really hard.
Every time I try to forget,
It would come back clearer,
Even clearer yet.
It will always be
In my heart,
And in my mind.

Tringa Dalladaku (11)
Holland Park School, Kensington & Chelsea

THIS IS FOOTBALL

Football is something that everybody likes
And I like it too.
I like it because my mum told me that my third name
Is a football name
This is the first thing
The second thing is that my dad is also a football player
And to show me that it was true
He showed me his picture.
That is why I like football so much.

Morel Groguhé (11)
Holland Park School, Kensington & Chelsea

DIFFERENT BY DAY

The day dawns and her hair flows out,
Golden and brown, down to her shoulders.
Eyes like chocolate, creamy and brown,
Skin so soft, like cotton wool, brown like her eyes.

Lips as full as summer rosebuds
Only peaceful words spoken.
She's the wonder of the land,
Secretive, but beautiful by day.

Night falls and her hair turns ebony
Matted and lifeless.
Her eyes turn a piercing hazel
And her nails grow into claws.
Black and aged.

Her lips make a frown,
Clothes like that of a funeral
But her words stay the same
Kind and beautiful, sharing wisdom with all.

Her looks may be different
But she's still the same
The curse of a witch will always remain.

Please do not judge her
She's just one of us.
By day or by night her heart stays the same.

Samara Edwards Amos (11)
Holland Park School, Kensington & Chelsea

AUTUMN

The trees are losing all their hair
I think they're dyeing it too,
I think they might have picked up
A very bad case of tree flu.

They've grown extremely long fingers,
Which reach into the night.
The bark has turned to monsters' mouths,
That look like they might bite.

The colours flash into existence,
Stumbling to the ground.
In the form of crispy leaves
Spiralling round and round.

Leaves continue to fall with the wind,
As the autumn months wear on.
They make nice patterns on the floor,
But soon they will be gone.

The autumn makes way for winter,
The leaves all vanish too.
Memories will be saved forever
Guy Fawkes has now burned through.

Tyrone Dunnill (13)
Holland Park School, Kensington & Chelsea

AUTUMN BLING

Autumn, winter, summer, spring
Autumn come
Autumn bling
Hot or cold, I can't tell
Leaves drop, flowers dwell.

Sooner or later autumn will end
While the weather mix and blend
Leaves are brown, orange and yellow
Trees just lay soft and mellow.

I don't know what autumn will bring
Hot or cold
Soon winter, soon spring
Right now it ain't so nice
Autumn catching like a vice.

Chad Solomon (13)
Holland Park School, Kensington & Chelsea

AUTUMN WINDS

In autumn, trees lose their leaves,
they fall off in the winter breeze.
They change from green to yellow to brown,
as they fall upon the ground.

So as the leaves fall from the trees,
they make space for brand new leaves.
After this the leaves begin to grow,
so now it's time for winter, which brings the snow.

And now it's a brand new season altogether,
The season of winter which brings the bad weather.

Katie Ellis (13)
Holland Park School, Kensington & Chelsea

AUTUMN LEAVES

Autumn leaves tumble down
like feathers to the ground,
Floating slowly down to Earth
and lying thoughtlessly on the turf.

Green, brown, yellow, orange and red
drifting quietly down on dying flower beds.
The sky seems to look dull and grey
in autumn, it looks like that nearly every day.

The trees look completely bare
with no leaves left to wear.
The trees look unhappy
the leaves look unhealthy,
everything seems to look gloomy
but still . . .
The autumn leaves tumble down
like feathers to the ground.
Floating slowly down to Earth
and lying carelessly on the turf.

Fahima Begum (14)
Holland Park School, Kensington & Chelsea

DREAMS (NIGHTMARES)

When you go to sleep at night
You soon wake up with a bit of a fright
As you sleep softly with grace
Your imagination takes you into a different place

In your head not everything is right
But what do you expect, it is at night
Yes, nothing is the same
Everything in your head is playing a game

What you see is very queer
And it is coming very near
What's the matter, you're not dismayed?
There is no time to be afraid.

Look! Watch out!
Don't start to scream and shout
'There, there!' your mum says
As you wake from your daze

Was it a dream or was it not?
In ten days time you would have forgot.

Nancy Dark Bukasa (11)
Holland Park School, Kensington & Chelsea

MY RABBIT FLUFFY

My pet rabbit Fluffy
She's one of those tuffys
I love her ears
she makes me shed tears
She's really friendly
When I'm angry
She makes me feel better
And I send her a 'thank you' letter
Her colourful coat feels like a sailing boat
I really like my Fluffy
I tell you she's one of those tuffys.

Leila Salouane (11)
Holland Park School, Kensington & Chelsea

THE POLICE VAN

They drag him to the police van
It was broad daylight
They kick him down the street
I knew it was not right
His nose had moved
It was an ugly sight
They beat him to make him still
But he put up a fight.

Remmel Shai Clarke (12)
Holland Park School, Kensington & Chelsea

THROUGH THE WIND

Walking through the wind
Rustling from the trees
Leaves fall with ease
They blow to and fro
And up they go
Spinning round and round
Then fall upon the ground
The sound of whistling beneath my feet
Oh, it makes me want to sleep
Goodnight!

Kelsey Louiese Hines (11)
Holland Park School, Kensington & Chelsea

RED

What is red?
Fire!
The burning anger inside of me.
Red is a warning, warning you away
Red is the danger you could come across
Red is blood, falling from a raw wound.
Red as eyes that have shed too many tears.
As red as a human heart, pumping blood.
Red as a rabbit's evil eyes, glaring at me

Hana Hersi (12)
Hornsey School For Girls, Hornsey

BULLY

His big body,
His fat face,
His big feet,
Shaking up the place.

Going up and down the streets,
Shouting at everyone he meets.

When his feet are bare, it stinks of cheese,
He probably has a foot disease.

Stupid at school,
He is a real big fool.

His hair is so picky,
His fingers are so sticky.

He acts all rough,
Isn't really tough.

Amina Rahmane (12)
Hornsey School For Girls, Hornsey

In Love

When you're in love your heart melts
like a pound of butter,
And your eyelids flicker and flutter
Your cheeks go red when you see that guy
he talks to you and you get all shy.
You're waiting for the special day
when lover boy will say
I love you!
And you reply *I love you too!*
You you'll tell everyone you're his girlfriend
And you'll love each other 'til the end.

Rashida Labrisi (11)
Hornsey School For Girls, Hornsey

THE FEELING

When you're about ten, you will feel
something that you have never felt before.

First you see someone, your heart begins to beat
faster and faster until butterflies take over your stomach.

Then you feel like being so friendly to that person
and you dream about them.

The next day, people are shouting out your name
saying how much you like that person,
but then you know that that feeling - is *love!*

Bianca Julien (11)
Hornsey School For Girls, Hornsey

PAIN

I'm in pain again,
You hurt me for the last time.
Falling down the stairs,
Breaking more than an arm.
Being in hospital
Seeing you visit and saying *sorry*.
It doesn't mean anything any more,
When you hurt me more than once,
I can't believe you when you say 'never again'.
I wish I was dead because of the way you make me feel.
Being here, lying there, being watched.
It's all your fault!

Louisa Emine Law (13)
Hornsey School For Girls, Hornsey

MY PETS

Silent pattering of tiny feet
Darting in and out of shadows
Looking here, looking there
Noses sniffing everywhere
Soft fur, sharp claws
Whiskers twitching, tickling
Bright eyes staring all around
Always making lots of sound
In and out of shadows they run
Hiding from their owner's glare
Scratching, washing, eating. What fun!
Making the scared ones run, run, run
The owners play, cuddle and hug
Feed them fruit, but only some
Their tails are strong, ridged and long
Hearts beat fast in rhythm to song
They run so fast, here and there
Clasping claws and teeth are long
My little friends I love so dear
If you did see them you'd never fear
Mimi and Precious are their names
Brown and white with large black eyes
Little nippers, but so sweet
My pet rats you have to meet.

Kelly Senior (14)
Hornsey School For Girls, Hornsey

LOVE

What is love?
An intense feeling,
A feeling of excitement and anxiety,
A feeling of hope and fear,
An excuse to be happy,
An excuse to be sad,
An excuse to dream
A very simple word,
But with lots of different meanings,
Is it a fantasy?
Have I reasons to believe?

Love exists within our hearts,
In mine and in yours,
Love is something we can't escape,
Love is something we can't always face,
Love is as sweet as honey,
But as sour as grapes.

Love is fair,
Love is foul,
Love treats you good,
Love treats you bad,
Love treats you the way you want it to,
But one thing is for sure,
Love is very true.

Namita Gupta (14)
Hornsey School For Girls, Hornsey

WHY ME?

I walk down the street
And wonder why they
Are staring at me.
Is it because I'm pretty,
Fat or ugly?
I think they are looking at me
Because I'm big.
I don't like the word fat,
It hurts my feelings.
It's not fair, why do they
Have to look at me?
They must be thinking,
Here comes a big fat whale.
'Oh no, earthquake!'
Instead of staring at me
Why don't you help me?
Why don't you put yourself
In my shoes for a day?
Then you'll see it's not
That easy to be me!

Sara-Jane Perryman (14)
Hornsey School For Girls, Hornsey

AS A BABY

Little world, new to me
A place where I can scream and scream.
Little happiness, lots of anger
Lust for strength, lust for power.
In this world of dark and storm,
I use my time to mourn and mourn.
Wishing I had the light again.
Praying I'll see it again.
Dreaming I'll feel it again.
Little world, new to me
A place where I can see and see.
See the frustration that I've caused.
When I was just their little good cause.
It's hard, it's pain
Pain drains and drains.
I'll never feel the same again.

Emma Kosminsky (14)
Hornsey School For Girls, Hornsey

MELTING POT DREAMS

Silver stars
fly by Mars.
Forty-two floating cats
become stripy bats.
Twisting, golden stairs,
lead to hairy bears.
Grabbing claws
act like saws.
And fairy dust
combusts.

Rebecca Wallwork (12)
Hornsey School For Girls, Hornsey

I Am Mixed

I am mixed,
Not black and not white.
So there is no need to fight,
Over which I belong,
Either one I'll stay strong.
I am mixed with two faces
And just because they're from different races,
Doesn't mean I am different from you
And no, I am not split in two
One half a different colour to the other,
That's not the way we're supposed to see each other.
We all have to look on the inside,
To find out all the things the outside hides.
To look beyond the colour of skin,
To find the person that's deep within
And even if you think I am strange,
Because my colour isn't fixed,
I don't care because I am proud of being mixed.

Lauren Andrew (14)
Hornsey School For Girls, Hornsey

IF I RULED . . .

If I ruled the world how would it change?
Would it get better, worse, or just stay the same?

Fights and war I would stop breaking out,
People would talk, not scream and shout.

I would give all the ordinary people a say,
Everyone together would decide the right way.

Racing would be about taking part
Not about winning to finish from start.
Ugly or pretty, thick or thin
Everybody is the same within.
Love and hate would still exist
But out of hate no one would use their fist.
Everything would cost what it's actually worth,
No child would be laboured for Nike from birth,
Dark or light, Asian, African or white
No one would have reason to fight.

Elly Beaman-Brinklow (14)
Hornsey School For Girls, Hornsey

MELODY OF THE WIND

Don't cry for me,
For I am fading,
Be happy and never give up,
Because I will always watch over you,
Always.
I don't feel much,
No more pain or sorrow,
I almost don't feel scared,
almost.
I will always miss the middle earth,
The grass,
The ever-flowing streams,
The trees,
The people, my friends.
But I'll also miss the wind,
I like the wind,
The way it used to blow roughly against my body,
Like invisible daggers that split into whiskers of gentle swirls when it
hits soft, gentle skin.
The way it used to brush against my face and the bangs of my hair,
floating them in the air as if by themselves.

When I was alone the wind was always there for me . . .
It made me feel free, safe, strong and ready to make anything possible,
If only for a short while.
When I'm gone from here will I ever feel the wind again?
My only roots are strength and hope. Or will it be taken away from me
like everything else that was ever dear and close to my heart?

I don't know now, for I'm fading. You have
shown me that there is a way to love and to cherish,
that I will never forget . . .

Like the wind,
Life will always come and go,
So fast,
You'll never realise how truly precious it really is. But it is my time
now, like it was for my ancestors and will be for you my friend,
I promise we'll meet again for I will be the melody of the wind.

Angelique Ibrahim (14)
Hornsey School For Girls, Hornsey

SLAUGHTER HOUSE

Picture perfect and perfectly sweet
Babies nestle at mothers' teats.
Brothers and sisters, all in a row,
Too bad that it's time to go.
Torn away by vicious hands,
Far too young to understand.
Cramped up in a dark, dank van,
Driven by a scary man.
Tossed around and bashed about,
Babies squeal, babies shout.
Doors are opened, there's the light,
Surely freedom is in sight?
But their journey isn't over, no,
Into the building they must go.
Babies in pens await their fates,
Bloody knives and Heaven's gates.

Evelyn Hughes (14)
Hornsey School For Girls, Hornsey

LOVE

Love!
What is the meaning of love?

Some people say you can't describe it,
Some say it's untouchable,
Some say it's painful,
Some say it's happiness,
Some say it's what keeps you alive.

The four words to describe love:

Painful, because you know that you're only
a step away from it, but can't go.

Happiness, because even if you can't go near it
the word itself keeps you alive.

Untouchable, because it's deep inside you
and never stops bleeding.

Life, because it's a way of living even if it's
painful, untouchable or sometimes deadly.

Love is the power that burns inside us
That's how it makes every single one of us
Different from each other.

Gulseren Kaya (15)
Hornsey School For Girls, Hornsey

REALITY

Door opens, in comes Dad,
Mum's face puffy, she is sad.
Argue, argue, shout, shout,
Me in bed thinking, what's it about?
The drama fades into a dim echo,
Leaving me with a soggy pillow.
Hate, love, fault, blame,
Is this real or is it a game?

Brother asks, 'What happened last night?'
'Did the cats have a fight?'
'Yes, Josh, but Gingy's fine.'
Just went to bed and did some cryin'
I knew, the cat was Mum,
I had sussed it out like a simple sum.
Hate, love, fault, blame,
Is this real or is it a game?

The truth hurts, what can we do?
It hurts when you know, 'Together, Forever' won't come true.
Pretend to lose Dad won't mean a thing,
Deny that this whole thing is not happening.
Just when I thought we were getting strong,
I look at my family, I was wrong.
Hate, love, fault, blame,
Is this real or is it a game?

Door slams shut, out storms Dad,
Mum's face red, she is mad.
Scream, scream, shout, shout.
I know exactly what it's all about.
The drama fades into a dim echo,
Leaving me with yet another soggy pillow
Hate, love, fault, blame,
This is real, not a game.

Nahide Ekim (14)
Hornsey School For Girls, Hornsey

FAIRIES

Angular ears and soft, long, flowing hair,
small pointy feet and skin colour fair.
Small silvery wings and elegant hands,
these are the creatures of Nowhere Land.

Dancing and singing, no work to be done,
the elders talk whilst the children have fun.
Each lives in a toadstool, bright red with white spots,
little doors and curtains tied together with knots.

A primitive lifestyle us humans might say,
to laugh and sing and joke and play.
But the Nowhere folk differ from you or I,
in ways you couldn't imagine, if you were to try.

They're carefree and joyful, they haven't a care,
no sickness or hunger, 'cause there's plenty to share.
No spiteful remarks or brawls on the street,
they accept every new person that they meet.

No religion or colours, just a community,
full of individuals, happy and free.
Nobody to tell you what's right or what's wrong,
they're not forced to change, so they all get along.

Each of them different, in face and in mind,
some funny, some cunning, but all of them kind.
Yet when there's a problem, they then all unite,
put brains together to set it right.

Each of them listens to what others say,
gather ideas and choose the right way.
There is no leader, no governing force,
the people decide, they choose the right course.

And so they are happy and so they should be
for even with all our computers and new technology.
We still have the homophobes, racists and bigots,
ask yourself, what could I change? Now answer it - lots.

Abigail Gledhill (14)
Hornsey School For Girls, Hornsey

ME, THE DRAGON AND THE DREAM

I had a dream,
Not a very nice one,
A big dragon,
Not a very friendly one,
It chased us,
It had long, sharp claws,
We ran.

There was a race,
Whoever reached the stairs,
Would be safe.
The stairs disappeared,
I was the *last*,
Only me and the dragon,
Me, who was in fear,
The dragon, fearless.

It reached out to grab me,
Long, sharp claws,
Standing there panicking,
I shut my eyes,
Then something went *bang!*
I opened my eyes,
I sat there shaking with horror.

Hat Thi Duong (12)
Hornsey School For Girls, Hornsey

FLOWER POWER

Flowers on the bedspread
Flowers on the wall
Flowers on the lampshade
Flowers overall.

Everything's so *nice*
Everything's so *girly*
Everything's so *pink!*
Like I'm meant to be *cute and curly.*

I wish it was like me
I wish it was normal
I wish it was classy
But nothing too formal.

The flowers are in power
Why can't they go away?
Why can't I have my room decorated?
Why can't I have my say?
Everywhere I look there's *flowers!*

Jade Tucker (12)
Hornsey School For Girls, Hornsey

SUMMER FUN

I need to find a hot spot
Where there must be a Topshop
I need to buy a crop top
To wear it at my hot spot!

I'm sitting at my hot spot
The burning, golden sand
Slipping through my toes
It feels like a soft, scarlet rose.

It's time to go . . .
I'm feeling so low
I was having so much fun
With the burning sun!

Janki Johri (12)
Hornsey School For Girls, Hornsey

PONY MAD

I am here to tell you about my hobby, horse riding.
There are lots of horses and ponies that I ride.
But I am here to tell you about the tricky things these ponies do.
Flambow is my favourite,
A very friendly steed.
He canters with his head down
And is very hard to please.

Casey causes trouble,
She is very strong.
She loves to jump at top speed
And that is so much fun.

Smithy is a real character,
He loves to run away,
Especially when you're on his back,
With no chance of getting away.
Habibi the most mysterious of all,
Always tries to buck you off,
Like a huge rocking horse,
In the hope that you will fall.
Now that you have heard my pony mad poem.
Which one would you choose?

Shalimar Hamilton-Edwards (12)
Hornsey School For Girls, Hornsey

MY DREAM

I awoke to hear a drama,
A man in shining armour,
I approached the stairs, to my surprise,
I saw a knight with big red eyes,
My heart went double *bam! Boom!*
I ran into the living room,
He chased me around and around,
Then I heard the clock sound,
I knocked over some chairs,
He marched back downstairs.

Jane Lant (12)
Hornsey School For Girls, Hornsey

NO MORE PAIN

Look around you and what do you see?
Murderers and people that look strange.
Pollution, things dying in wars and abuse
But we can make a change.

Feel around you and what do you feel?
Heat from fires and weapons that are out of their range.
Pain from being attacked or pushed
But don't feel sad we can make a change.

Listen around you and what do you hear?
Arguments and swear words from each lane.
People screaming, crying for help
So let's all come together and make a change
And have *no more pain.*

Genevieve Harrison (12)
Hornsey School For Girls, Hornsey

THE WAR

One of the best days of the week, Saturday.
But not a very good one.
Eleven hot, sunny days.
Every morning you wake up,
You feel scared and sad.

You could smell the smell of the war.
You want to go out and have fun with your friends,
But you can't because you're so scared
Of what's going to happen to you
You think someone might take you away
And something will happen really bad to you.

You're at home every minute of every day.
You haven't got anything to do.
You try to think of something, but you can't
Because you're completely lost.

So you go to sleep.
Thinking what's going to happen tomorrow?
When you wake up on the eleventh day,
You find out that you have to leave home
And go to Macedonia because of the war.
You think you're going to die, but in the end you're safe.

Alketa Berisha (12)
Hornsey School For Girls, Hornsey

MY WEIRD NIGHTMARE

I hope they still like me
I hope they're still the same
But the madness must remain.

I hope they don't get cross . . . cross
Especially Ross . . . Ross
I'm excited, but scared . . . scared
Help me, I'm lost . . . lost!

I'm lost in this nightmare . . . nightmare
No one cares less . . . less
I think I'm losing my rag . . . rag
I'm in such a mess . . . mess
Help me, I'm lost!

Being lost is quite scary
Oh so scary
I'm lost in this nightmare
Help me, please.

I weep and weep
I keep no secrets in my sleep
Even in a *nightmare!*

Gemma D'Olivera (12)
Hornsey School For Girls, Hornsey

THE CHOCOLATE TWIRL

I had a dream,
It may sound strange,
I was in a shop buying chocolate,
Yum!
It was a Twirl, my favourite,
I opened the wrapper as slowly as I could,
When I finished opening my Twirl,
I was getting ready to put it in my mouth,
I could feel the warm, melting chocolate about to fall into my mouth,
Then I suddenly heard my alarm clock and woke up,
So at the end,
I didn't get to taste my Twirl after all.

Karla Jones (12)
Hornsey School For Girls, Hornsey

THE ENVIRONMENT

The environment,
Keep it clean,
The environment,
You know what I mean.

Don't use spray cans
On the wall,
Don't draw graffiti
On the wall.

Don't cut down trees,
Animals' habitats,
You're harming helpless birds and bees,
Instead recycle.

Care for nature,
It cares for you,
It's the future
And you are too.

Kimberley Linyard-Tough (12)
Hornsey School For Girls, Hornsey

COLOUR

The colour is yellow,
The colour is green,
The colour is all that we have seen,
The colour is blue as the bluebells spring,
Yes! The colours of spring.

Spring is the beginning,
The beginning of life,
As the birds' songs of dawn are ringing,
From treetop to steeple, joy they are bringing,
Yes! The colours of spring.

The colour is yellow,
The colour is blue,
The colours are many, not few,
The colour is the flowers, the flowers of summer,
Yes! The colours of summer.

As spring dies away,
Summer comes bringing the bright, summer sun,
For summer has its joys,
The seaside, the holidays, the noise
Yes! The colours of summer.

The colour is orange,
The colour is brown,
The colours are like the great king's crown,
The colour is the leaves, the golden-coloured leaves,
Yes! The colours of autumn.

Autumn is here, summer's no more,
The nights draw in like a mighty lion's roar,
The leaves fall away
And we must all say that autumn isn't here to stay,
Yes! The colours of autumn.

The colour is white,
The colour is red,
The colours are simply not dead,
The colour is snow, it's our friend not our foe,
Yes! The colours of winter.

Winter is here, but we must not fear,
For spring is soon to come,
But in the meantime Santa is to come
Bringing joy like the bright summer sun.
Yes! The colours of winter.

Ann Gallagher (13)
Hornsey School For Girls, Hornsey

NEVER STOP

Never stop loving yourself
Never stop believing in yourself
You gotta take yourself for who you are
You gotta tell yourself you are who you are
Never stop and wait for others to lift you
Never stop and say I'll never deserve to . . .
You gotta reach the unexpected
You gotta spread the talents in you
Never stop trying, trying as you'll ever
Never stop building, building more of what you have
You gotta find your inner beauty
You gotta search for your deeper stories, but
Never stop loving yourself and
Never stop believing in yourself.

Omolabake Odushegun (13)
Hornsey School For Girls, Hornsey

ANGEL OF DEATH

Bitter-sweet love.
The gash in my heart.
My living, my being,
My all.

I feed off the air you breathe,
The sanctuary you weave.
Your burning eyes stare,
Deep into my soul.

I shall one day have my love.
You won't just be in photos
Plastered all over my wall
All over my mind
But here, with me.

I know you will come,
It's just a matter of time.
I know your feelings are the same,
That hiding them is a strain.

They have to be
Stop staring at me!
Spying, surrounded, suffocating
So cold, so blank, so empty,
Just like me.

I will be your angel of death
Your saviour, your god
The bomb I send for you
The death I cause for me.

And you shall come to see
Us up there together
As we are meant to be.

Caitlin Clunie O'Connor (13)
Hornsey School For Girls, Hornsey

SHHH!

I go to a place
I don't know where
When I'm sad
And they don't care
I go on my own
Because I have the key
I open the door
To my fantasy
It's my little secret
And nobody knows
Except for me
And the reader I chose
When I go there
I can scream and shout
And say all the things
I want to let out
When I'm there
It goes so fast
But when I return
I return to the past
I go to a place
I don't know where
I know I should
But I don't want to share
Shhh!

Lisa Gilby (14)
Hornsey School For Girls, Hornsey

MY PAIN

I have my own box,
Inside it I hide my pain,
I try to get away
From the trouble on my mind that day.

Only me and my thoughts know what I'm feeling,
Right now I feel like dying,
The pain, the anger, it's killing,
What should I really be feeling?

I think I'm losing my mind,
I think I'm going mad,
This all feels so bad
Why is no one being kind?

I wish it would all go away,
I wish I could hide the pain,
Right now I feel so dead,
Right now I feel so dead.

I have my own box,
Inside it I hide my pain,
I try to get away
From the trouble on my mind that day.

Shima Khabazan (13)
Hornsey School For Girls, Hornsey

WATER

The water it drips, drips
As it hits the ground
It rings, rings
Like a wet finger on a crystal glass
The music it makes, it sings, sings.
The dribbles they squiggle, squiggle
Through the grooves of the rock
They move, move
Then they meet at the bottom
And turn into a stream
And onto the river
They groove, groove.
The river it swirls, it swirls
It winds like a snake
It rushes, rushes
It jumps and it dives
But stays going on
And on to the sea, it gushes, gushes.
The sea it waves, waves
It circles about so fast, fast
Like the sands of time through the hourglass
It drips from the future to the past, past.

Raina vonAhn (11)
Hornsey School For Girls, Hornsey

SOME OF US ARE DIFFERENT

Some of us are different
Unique you may say
So unique they have to be made fun of
Picked on and bullied
They're ordinary
Just like you and I
So why do they have to be tortured
For no reason at all?
They have equal rights
Don't destroy them just because you feel they're different
Have you ever thought
That *you* may be different and you don't know it?
Next time before you decide to make a judgement
Look in the mirror
You just may be the one that's different.

Toyin Adebiyi (13)
Hornsey School For Girls, Hornsey

AS THE YEARS GO PAST THINGS CHANGE

As the years go past things change,
As the day goes past people say,
That the day is not the same,
As it was the other day.

If I say it scientifically,
The brain decides to go swiftly,
Into its own little room,
That only exists in dreams.

I hear people say that if I go my way,
I would become who I want to be,
The person people want to see
But as the day goes by that person will die.

Sometimes regret, sometimes agreed,
Sometimes you will want more of life to be seen,
In your little room, that only exists in dreams.

Pelin Duran (13)
Hornsey School For Girls, Hornsey

WHO IS HE?

Who is he?
I saw him once among the autumn leaves
Who is he?
I heard him once, the soft way he breathes.

Who is he?
I felt him once, his fingers through my hair
Who is he?
I smelt him once, his lavender perfume in the air.

Who is he?
The one who walks so elegantly
Who is he?
The one with eyes so heavenly.

When will I have the one I love?
I ask you, oh great One above.

Fazeelat Mirza (13)
Hornsey School For Girls, Hornsey

GREEN

(Based on the poem Yellow by Helen Dunmore)

Think of something green.
The grass,
The leaves on a tall, healthy tree
Or a bitter apple.

Green is jealousy,
Green is an emerald,
Green is my best friend's eyes.

Green is Brussel sprouts which all parents try
To make their children eat.
Green is the man in the traffic light
Allowing you to cross the road.
Green . . . is my favourite colour.

Deychen Wangmo (13)
Hornsey School For Girls, Hornsey

THE DAY HAS BEGUN
(Based on the poem Night and Stars)

The light of the day
The night's gone astray
In from the sun
The day has begun.

Farzaana Yunus Mussa (13)
Hornsey School For Girls, Hornsey

RED

(Based on the poem Yellow by Helen Dunmore)

Red
Think of something red.
Fire?
Blood?
Red ink?

Red is a strawberry
Red is a cherry
Red is meat
What is red?

Red is my mum's sparkling jewellery box.
So bright it shocks your eyes.
The glittery rings and ruby-red earrings.
Red is the colour of the precious little book
I put my thoughts in.

Fahmida Begum Hussain (12)
Hornsey School For Girls, Hornsey

PURPLE HEART

Lavender,
My pencil case or my bedroom
Purple is a plum
A beetroot
An aubergine.

Purple, my CD player
My favourite photo
My favourite jumper.

Purple is all my happy feelings
Purple is the colour of my heart.

Miriam Zaatri (12)
Hornsey School For Girls, Hornsey

LOST

I lost my penny
I lost my dime
I lost my watch
And couldn't tell the time.

I lost my slippers
I lost my shoes
I couldn't wear my knickers
Cause I lost them too.

I lost my jacket
I lost my hat
I lost my jumper
And couldn't wear that.

I got so angry
I lost my head
Mum got mad
And sent me to bed.

Sehar Siddiqui (12)
Hornsey School For Girls, Hornsey

TWO INCHES AWAY FROM DANGER

I'm two inches away from danger,
An explosion nearby,
I feel as if there's a stranger,
That is waiting for me to die,
I know it's a horrible feeling,
But that's what I feel inside.
The explosion keeps on rising,
As I run fast it gets faster,
The glow from it was shining,
The pain could not be hidden by a plaster.
But something swung my neck
And pulled me in!
I screamed, 'Oh heck!'
I ran, trying to avoid that pain in my shin,
It might have been the stranger,
Who tried to put me in danger!
But I run out of town for good,
Or I might be two inches away from danger once more.

Sonia Lassami (12)
Hornsey School For Girls, Hornsey

LOVE

Love makes me feel wanted.
Love is as sweet as honey.
Love makes people get closer.
When I think about love it melts me down.
Love tastes like strawberries.
The word love makes me feel warm and happy!

Sobika Somasundaram (12)
Hornsey School For Girls, Hornsey

DRAGONS

Dragons eat anything or anyone,
Dragons, they have lots of fun.
They breathe puffs of smoke,
It makes people choke.
As they lazily lie down
Guarding jewels or maybe a crown.
Would you dare?
Would you go there?

Alice Mary Bell (11)
Hornsey School For Girls, Hornsey

ALL ABOUT ME

R achel, that's my name

A lways playing a game

C ynthia, that's my mum

H appy when I'm doing something fun

E verlasting love I'll love my family until then

L ovely because I'm a gem

B enjamin that's a very popular name (it's my surname)

E ternity, I'll love my mum until I die

N othing, that's what I do in my spare time

J oel, he's my brother

A mazing, that's what I am

M onique, she is my sister

I nventing, I love making new things

N ever ever wanting to die.

That's what I can say about me.

Rachel Benjamin (11)
Hornsey School For Girls, Hornsey

PEACE VS WAR

The world is made up of my two countries.
One is good and fights for peace,
The other's bad, bad and mean.
Number one shouts things like peace and love,
As for the other one, hates the above.
I wish my world would shape up a bit
So war would end and peace would stick.

Anna Babic (11)
Hornsey School For Girls, Hornsey

I AM AN OCTOPUS

I am an octopus,
With eight slithering tentacles,
I live in the sea,
When I get hurt I can't go to hospital.

On my tentacles I have suckers,
So I can stick, stick anywhere,
Humans eat octopuses,
But I'm poisonous, so I'm rare!

I eat lots of things,
Like crabs, starfish and mussels,
I grab them and jump on them,
They're so frightened I poke them just like pencils.

Monira Sirazam Ali (11)
Hornsey School For Girls, Hornsey

MY BEAUTIFUL GARDEN

Come and see my beautiful garden.
We will have loads of fun,
Playing in the bright green grass
Just you and me in the sun.

We can play with my rabbits
And even find my cat.
If you don't like that well . . .
You can borrow Dad's funny hat.

I think you will enjoy it
Though it's hard to say
Because I've never had a special friend
To play with on a sunny day.

Come back and play another day
We can pick flowers for hours and hours.
I'm glad we had a fantastic day
You're my friend and here to stay.

Karys McDermott (11)
Hornsey School For Girls, Hornsey

CRY WHALE, CRY!

Cry whale, cry!
Just like the moaning
Ocean weeping with you.

Cry whale, cry!
Just like the lonely
Shark hunting for its perilous prey.

Cry whale, cry!
Just like the hungry
Waves have no time to stay.

Cry whale, cry!
Just like the shy
Dolphin waiting for its life to
Be taken away.

Cry whale, cry!
Just like the sorrowful
Sea horse gliding along.

Cry whale, cry!
For if not, the ocean
Will vanish!

Kauthar Siddique Parkes (12)
Hornsey School For Girls, Hornsey

WHAT IS RED?
(Based on the poem Yellow by Helen Dunmore)

Think of something red
Love
Roses
Blood.

Red is danger
Red is power
Red is fire
What is red?

The colour red is what you can see
The colour red is what you see when you fall to the ground.
Red is a poppy in its barley bed.

Lauren Scanlon (11)
Hornsey School For Girls, Hornsey

LIFE

What is life?
The life we lead
The life we love, hate and live.

Try to explain life!
You can't, life is:
One of those things,
You know those things
You can't touch it,
You can't see it,
You can't hug it.

Life
Life is happy,
Sad,
Fantastic,
Shy

Life
Life is unique to everyone
Life is itself.

Alice Johns (11)
Hornsey School For Girls, Hornsey

TV

Think about something on TV
Emmerdale?
Coronation Street?
Brookside?

TV is something you enjoy looking at.
TV is my life and if you think about it
I live with it, mostly in the evenings.
TV is something that doesn't bore you,
Certainly not me.
Anyone who doesn't like TV
They shouldn't be living,
TV is really my life
And I'll never *give it up!*

Shazeda Uddin (11)
Hornsey School For Girls, Hornsey

GREEN

Think of something green,
The grass?
The leaves?
The pond?

Green is a gel-pen
Green is a juicy apple
Green is Shikira's pencil case.

What is green?
Green are the leaves of the trees that give oxygen
Green is the colour of nature
Green is the natural world where the wild creatures live.

Kadijah Congoma (11)
Hornsey School For Girls, Hornsey

OUR BRAND NEW SCHOOL

'We welcome you to a whole new school
Don't destroy it, it's a happy day,
With this new school there's some whole new rules
That will keep you on your way.'
After this day I found some things I liked and I would like to say:
The facilities are great,
They go with the gate,
It's hard to find your way,
I love the computers with plasma screens,
The toilets are as clean as slate,
There's no gum anywhere,
If there is people stare,
For it's all so rare nowadays.
Instead people love the cool new school and its pleasant atmosphere,
That's the end of our tour of the cool new school,
Thanks for coming here!

Tamir Jacob (12)
JFS School, Kenton

DEAR MY LOVE

Dear my love

The time has come for me to express how I feel,
Your beauty is spectacular, radiant, unreal,
You're as pretty as a flower and a rose,
That's why I have to tell you something no one else knows,
It may come as a shock, but it's time for me to tell,
I love you so much; you've caught me under your spell,
All day I dream about your pretty eyes,
So radiant they are like stars from the sky,
I love you, I adore you, I really do,
No one can change my feelings for you,
I love the way you curl up your hair,
Your looks are so pretty, no one can compare,
Your face is as stunning as the sea,
I'm now going down onto one knee,
I love you, I love you, I really do,
So please don't hurt me, say *I do.*

Daniel Navazesh (14)
JFS School, Kenton

MY LOVE FOR YOU

My sweet you are an angel,
An angel from above,
To share all of your beauty,
Is what I'm dreaming of.

For years I have been searching,
For a love so sweet and true,
But never have I found someone,
As warm and kind as you.

Your eyes are like the morning sun,
That illuminate my life,
To me you are more beautiful,
I wish you were my wife.

A phone call a day is not enough,
To show how much I care,
To see your face is all I wish,
And know you're always there.

I end these words with just one thought,
Which I hope you'll keep near your heart,
I love you so dearly, more than life itself,
And to think this is just the start.

David Scott (15)
JFS School, Kenton

LET'S PRAY IT STAYS

'What's the meaning of this?' he asks.
It means the light's working even when it's dark.

That doesn't answer anything
Why is this happening?
We were wrong and now we're being corrected
We almost had it taken away
Let's pray it stays.

If we learn from our mistakes and not do them again
Nothing bad will happen and we will have time to regain.
What happens if we do lose it though
If we feel like we will never see it again.
You have to be wrong to lose it.
If you are right, it will stay.

What if . . .
What if we lose it?
You remember what it was like when you still had it
Look for the positive and ask who gave it to you?
And who took it away?

Gideon Katzenberg (14)
JFS School, Kenton

CRIME

The dark is near
The cruel are calmly waiting
Their scars from past threats cast a shadow on their devilish faces
The kind go out and the unfeeling come in
Walking
Stalking
And yet you can't see them
Black as the night sky
Hoping for success
Pointless as their own freedom
They are like this thing
That loves and cares in the day
Then when the sun sets below its amber horizon
They turn into this beast that lurks around in the shadow of night
They walk on air
Not a foot seems to touch the ground
Taking from the rich
Keeping it for themselves
Dragging their heavy sacks to their hideouts
As the bright, golden sun breaks out from its lonely cage
They slither away like snakes
Not a soul shall ever know their identity.

Natan Rifkin (13)
JFS School, Kenton

THE STALKERS OF THE NIGHT

T he stalkers prowl the New York streets
H oping to find a bite to eat
E ven in the gloom the creepers gleam

S ome hunt them down until they scream
T he shout of fear they love to hear
A ll fall at last to their sick hands of darkness
L ike the evil in their hands they harness
K ing of the night, on their throne they lie low,
E vil is not man's greatest foe
R eally man pursues the night
S ickness and the need to fight

O nly we can see through stalker's eyes
F or inside us all a stalker lies

T hen waiting for the time to strike
H olding on and growing till the night
E ven tucked in our beds so tight

N astily crawl from our dreams
I nto the darkness the shadow leans
G rasping, crushing the holy light
H oping to banish her from the night
T omorrow though is a brand new day.

All the shadows now have slipped away
Banished back from the light of day
And in ourselves the demon sleeps
For another night they will come to creep.

David Meyer (13)
JFS School, Kenton

DAY AT SCHOOL

Monday morning,
School bell rings.
Talking to my friends,
Football team wins.
Get into the classroom,
Unpack our bags.
Teacher tells us our faces are tired and sad.
Finally lunchtime,
The smell of the food,
Students pushing,
Being rude.
Out in the playground,
Time to rest,
It's ever so cold,
Wear a vest.
Now it's last lesson
Think it's maths
Finding it a bit hard, got the hang of it!

Finally, home time . . .
Time to run out.

Ben Lassman (13)
JFS School, Kenton

AURORA

Gazing deep into the setting azure sky
Waiting for the sun to reappear up high,
Watching as shooting stars take a daring race
As the moon submerges and sun takes its place.

I wish these magnificent days never to end
But then I would never see dawn again
I would never see the dazzling sun rise
As it embarks on its passage through the infinite sky.

Your name, Aurora, goddess of the dawn.
Who brings end to night, the start of morn.
Reaching up high, conducting the sun, moon and stars,
To make the mortals and gods have light near and far.

The saffron-robed sun floating in the deep blue sky
The silver-lined moon among the diamonds up high
Two sisters who have never known that is who they are
Every day they come so close, yet they are so far.

If they met they would never part and this way they'd stay
Conjuring up a day that is night and a night that is day.
The sun and moon do not know who they are at dawn or dusk,
Oblivious of whom they pass, as they do what they must.

Thank you god of dawn who brings the beginning of light
and end to dark.
As the crimson sun is revealed, the start of the new day is marked.
The refreshing dawn chorus and the dew-dropped petals
bring joy and mirth.
The day brings mystery so we tread softly as if it is the first.

Danielle Oxenham (14)
JFS School, Kenton

TIGER OF THE NIGHT

Tiger of the night stealing through forests
Dark and warm
Smell the demon
The banded knight
His fur, thick, invisible, deadly
His claws curved.

His teeth bared
His eyes ever still
Tiger, tiger of the night.

Gazelle lie still
For I shall send you to the forest of eternal darkness
Like all who enter my vice-like jaws
Tiger, tiger of the night.

The chase begins, a mortal battle of the fates
The claws come down
The neck goes snap!
Gazelle's eyes are in the mist of death
The battle of the fates is won by the tiger of the night.

José D Silver (12)
JFS School, Kenton

THE LAST PETAL

A finger full of dust,
Spread on piles high.
Boxes of heels and buckles
And lavish ballgowns lie.

Embroidered ballerinas
A castle made of thread,
Bright flamenco dancers,
Forever blooms in red.

The warmth of sunlight lingers
Apples scattered around
But the roses never wither
'Til the last petal's found.

Amanda Wayne (14)
JFS School, Kenton

THE DREAMER

We have no time to run a distance,
To walk or talk, to make a difference.

We cannot waste our lives on dreaming,
We are told to stop, but I can't stop feeling
And wanting that breath of imagination.
Entering a world of mystification.
Believing the impossible and seeing the invisible,
Instead of an entire life of being miserable.
Leaving this cursed and doomed reality,
That's my speciality.

Living a life of loneliness and despair,
I find there's nothing worse, it's not fair,
Not to experience the passion and the yearn,
To love someone and be loved in return.
It's a shame when people hide behind their smile,
Their angelic faces make them feel vile.
Disguising your identity can truly get one down,
Spending eternity suffering in a ghost town.

We have no time to run a distance,
To walk or talk, to make a difference.

Claudia Cramer (13)
JFS School, Kenton

MY CAT

My cat, silky, soft and sleek he curls around my feet . . .
Time to go out, O'Mally,
Come on,
Do not be scared,
Come out of the door.

The door goes bang,
The lock goes click,
It's time for hunting,
Once again the cat is on the prowl,
Suddenly a dog goes *woof!*
O'Mally turns around,
He curves his back
And flashes his tail from side to side,
He hisses
And runs quietly into the night.

Then he spots it,
He stops,
Looks,
He hides and then . . .

Pounces!

Bird killed, O'Mally got it.

Now waiting on the step,
I open the door,
'Why have you got feathers in your mouth O'Mally?'
'It's a long poem,' he replies.

Rebecca Goodall (11)
La Sainte Union Convent School, Camden

CHILDREN AROUND THE WORLD

There are different kinds of children,
Who live around the world
Some children live in huts,
Some children live in cold igloos,
Others live in houses,
While others live on boats.
But it really doesn't matter,
As long as they are healthy, happy and good.
Some children are brown,
Yellow, black or white.
Their colours are different
But they are children like us.
Hear them laugh
And see them play.
Yes, they're only children,
But they have something to say.

Nesrin M Vural (12)
La Sainte Union Convent School, Camden

MY AUNTY JULIA

I love my aunty with all my heart
and would never like us to be apart.
Once she won a VIP day,
but being kind is just her way.

My aunty is the best by far,
because she is a shining star.
She always tries to look her best
and I bet she'd win a beauty contest!

My aunty is so very funny,
she likes it best when it is sunny.
My aunty she is so very strong,
if one thing was to go wrong with her strength,
she wouldn't weep long.

Eleanor Ashley (11)
La Sainte Union Convent School, Camden

WHERE ARE YOU?

Through the crowds I look for you
Where are you?
You seem to have so many back of the head twins
But when they turn round you're not there.
Where are you?
I get my hopes up but you're not there.
I look places you said I could find you
But you're not there.
You used to send cards and ring once in a while,
Never now.
I speak to you in my prayers, hoping you'll reply soon.
I wish I could find you.
I'd love to see you but you don't ever come.
It is stupid to remember things that happened long ago,
To remember what happened in the past.
Will my prayers soon be answered or any time at all?
Why have you gone so far away is what I want to know.
Everybody liked you, why did you have to leave?
My mind lost your picture long, long ago
But in my heart you're not forgotten
And will live on forever.
Come back and say goodbye.

Katherine Wise (11)
La Sainte Union Convent School, Camden

SWIMMING POEM

When I go swimming
It is not hot but cold.
I see the beautiful
Glazing water calling
For me to swim.
I dive in and see the beautiful
Faces reflecting around me.
I feel like a dolphin in the
Wonderful ocean.
I can feel the marvellous
Water rushing through my hair.

Sadie McMahon (12)
La Sainte Union Convent School, Camden

THE NIGHT

The pale moonlight shines on the shadows of the night
and dances with all its desire.
The highway twists and turns in the darkness
and the highwayman awakes to his destiny.
He strides around on horseback, the horse called Devil
With great red fiery burning eyes that stare into
The dark, black night.
The twinkling stars twinkle for their lives
for not to be swallowed by the monstrous night.
Shutters clatter in the wind and purple velvet and silk
curtains dance in the night.
Jewels, jewelled like melted merchandise
around the rim.

Rossana Duarte (11)
La Sainte Union Convent School, Camden

LIFE IS A GOOD THING

Life is a good thing, don't throw it away
For you see tomorrow is another day.

I love my life, it's the best thing around
From the moment I opened my eyes my feet touched the ground.

Some people don't like to be alive
But I really like it, especially when I was five.

I have parents to love and care for me
I will always love this you see.

Come on world, cheer up and keep your pace
I just wish I could see a happy face.

I just hope, after this
They will put down their fist
And make it better by giving friendship a kiss.

Karen Afriyie (11)
La Sainte Union Convent School, Camden

THE TIGER'S HEART

Deep
inside the tiger's
heart was a caring and
loving and elegant creature who
put the world of cats before him. When
they had prey he would wait to the end
and eat the little of what was left. One
night the tiger passed away. When
the world of cats awoke they
found the dead body and
the spirit said, 'Bury me
where the sun always shines
and the rain always falls
deep inside your hearts
and there I will always
remain.'

Ilda Abi-Khalil (11)
La Sainte Union Convent School, Camden

LOVE

Love is kind-hearted,
Love is patience,
Love is kindness,
Love is devotion,
Love is honesty,
Love is compassion,
Love is joy and love is faithfulness,
Love is the greatest gift,
Love is a commandment,
Love is understanding,
Love is a man's sign, a man's name,
Give to him by God,
Love draws two near,
Draws them near in perfect love
Which casts out fear.
Love joins them in communion here,
Love shall be our token,
Love be yours and love be mine,
Love for plea and gift and sign,
Richer than gold is the love of a man,
Better than splendour and wealth.
Love, only love is the key.

Barbara Achiaa-Yeboah (12)
La Sainte Union Convent School, Camden

THE GREAT SHINING MOON

Moving along looking at me,
knowing that I can see,
he shines down with lots of desire,
like the sun shining fire.

The moonlit trees are glittering,
as we hear the stars sing,
the night is really very dark,
as it has such a spark.

Grey mist passes slowly so,
giving it a great big glow,
its colour is so very clear,
that everyone might just fear.

So as I watch it with its light,
shining very big and bright,
in the distance far away,
he would never speak or say.

He follows me everywhere I go,
never thinking high or low,
look at his pale, white face,
not speeding up, just takes his pace.

In the morning I look to the sky,
all the way very high,
but I see the sun.

Where is the moon?

Rachel Fernandez (11)
La Sainte Union Convent School, Camden

TIME TO HEAL

I think of a time,
When loneliness no more,
Shall take a hold on me
And come knocking at my door.

A time that we thought that life was fun,
For some of us it still is,
But others still think,
Of a time we wept,
For the understanding of dreams.

We wept for understanding,
From those who didn't believe,
We wept for hope and peace and love,
We wept for time to grieve.

That time will come for me,
One day I know it will,
But until that day,
I have to say,
Enough of this misery.

Kemi Odunlami (12)
La Sainte Union Convent School, Camden

A Visit To The Forest

The sunlight sifts through the trees,
I hear the constant buzz of bumblebees,
In Toadstool Palace pixies wait for me,
I come inside for tea and pixie muffins,
After, we all go hunting for clovers.
But when all the fun is over,
I must go home to Dover.

Ella Godsell (11)
La Sainte Union Convent School, Camden

SCHOOL

Welcome to secondary school,
Welcome to a new world.

You're in trouble, no you're in big trouble.
You've managed to lose your geography and maths books
And your table's covered in books!
The zip on your pencil case is broken
And your lunch box has gone for a walk!
You haven't finished your history or French homework
And on top of that you haven't tidied your room
And Granny's coming round tonight!

Welcome to secondary school,
Welcome to a new world.

Andrea Ochaya (11)
La Sainte Union Convent School, Camden

FRIENDS

F   is for friends, we stick with each other.
R   is for relationships, there are all different kinds.
I   is for ice cream we share with each other.
E   is for enjoyment when we meet each other.
N   is for neighbours they can become good friends.
D   is for dearest, you are my dearest friend.
S   is for special, you are special to me.

Stacia Murphy (11)
La Sainte Union Convent School, Camden

September 11th

I go outside and see them cry,
as they look up into the sky.
Everybody seemed to see,
what has happened except for me.
Then I remember that dreaded date,
what happened and ended in so much fate.
I look at my calendar and just can't bear
what I see written there.
It is the day when the aeroplanes crashed,
it is the day when the towers smashed.
September 11th is the day
when everybody starts to pray.

Gemma Orchard (11)
La Sainte Union Convent School, Camden

9/11

To dream to fly is to dream to achieve
Did those who hijacked the planes achieve?
To cause death, destruction, misery and pain,
That day so many lives were slain.
Mothers, fathers, sons and wives,
For what reason did they lose their lives?
New Yorkers watched as the towers fell
Inside too many lives to tell.
Firemen rushed in ready to fight
Ready to die for what's just and right.
Died saving others - a hero's death
So little saved, saved before their very last breath.
Kids without parents, mums without daughters
Lives incomplete after all the slaughters.
In an empty house an answerphone says,
'Luv ya honey, see ya at eight.'
Not knowing at all it would be too late.
Mothers, fathers, husbands and wives
All dead for nothing, all of it lies.
Lovers embraced in a final kiss
Regretting a future they know they will miss.
Millions of people - candles in hand
Pray for the planes that did not come to land.

Marie-Claire Chappet (13)
La Sainte Union Convent School, Camden

THE CORN MOON'S FEAST

'Twas a dark night and a moonlit sky,
no one stirring, no bodies pass by,
except for a young girl all dressed in black,
holding a book and a small black cat.

She hears a sound of flapping wings,
a beast from the heavens and the treasure it brings.
She gleams at its scales, its sharp, scratchy claws,
hovering around on its all-fours.

Alas, 'tis a dragon standing proud and tall,
its wings spread freely like a waterfall.
Its eyes were red and scales were long,
scattering like the blue moon's song.

The young girl pats the dragon's prickly nose,
she is a witch of which nobody knows.
She climbs on the back of the homely beast,
awaiting her flight from the corn moon's feast.

Nicola Tozzi (12)
La Sainte Union Convent School, Camden

SUMMER THOUGHTS

A time to spend with family
Shopping trips with friends
Reading and relaxing
Lazing on a sandy beach
Ice creams galore
Sleepover parties
Swimming in the ocean
Holiday houses, usually empty,
Now are filled with laughing children.

Leah Breindel (9)
Lubavitch Senior Girls' School, Hackney

THE ARGUMENT

The cold, bitter look in her cold, bitter eyes
The wrong and the worry of what has been said
The quivering, cold, looming tension
The cruel thoughts whirling inside each head.

The dark, evil glances between one and the other
The slow building up to the final last straw
The icily, glare-spoken snapwords
The anger and hatred grow more.

The snapping and sneering and no longer caring
The tension replaced with scorn-glaring hate
The boiling of tempers as overflow spills
The nightmarish end to a nightmarish wait.

Emma Jourdan (11)
St Paul's Girls' School, Brook Green

CROCODILE

Lying low
Still as a statue
Watching, waiting
Hoping to catch you.

Down to the water
Down for a drink
Unsuspecting
Not stopping to think

From the water he darts
With a glint in his eyes
And again without sound
Disappears with his prize

Lying low
Still as a statue
Watching, waiting
Hoping to catch you.

Sophie Stephenson-Wright (11)
St Paul's Girls' School, Brook Green

FRIENDS

When I play with my friend
We wish play time will never end
Together my friend and me
We have cake and a tea
When we are in school
We think it's rather cool
Friends stay together forever
Forever and ever.

Simon Muhammad (11)
Sybil Elgar School, Ealing

I WANT TO BE A STAR

When I grow up
I want to be a star
And I will work in star films
And I will win an Oscar prize
I will sing in a musical
Dressed in pink and wearing gloves
I will dance to the music
I'll be on the stage
The audience will clap
I will be a star!

Melanie Hughan (15)
Sybil Elgar School, Ealing

Too Alone To Think Of A Title

Being a haunted house ain't fun
I used to be a house for goodwill nuns
Goodwill nuns who loved me so
I started to kill, they decided to go.

I stand here waiting for thee
But I can't bear the staring trees
I wish someone would forgive me
I know they won't, I killed half the county.

I'll stand here till death do us part
Please someone have a change of heart
This isn't funny I wait so long
The county starts to make up a song
About the idiot who doesn't realise
Half the county despises him.

But I still won't change
Their insults are out of my range
Silly tramps kick stones at me
I'll get my own back one day.

I am the haunted house
Who even mayors despised
But they don't realise I kill and kill
But why do I kill, how could this be?
I, in fact, am the soul of this stupid county.

Leonard Lewis (11)
Woodside Park International School, Barnet

THE LOCAL PARK

One hot summer's day
I went outside to play
When running around the local park
It suddenly got very dark
Five minutes later it poured with rain
So I ran home down the lane.

Chloe Bookatz (11)
Woodside Park International School, Barnet

THE TREE

I see you standing there,
throughout the years you grow and grow,
but never get anywhere,
you wave your branches through the air,
with the help of your friend the wind,
oh dear!

When I look out the window
you simply stand and stare,
when I look at you, leaves fall like newborn
feathers floating to the ground,
which means autumn's coming around.

Then it comes to winter,
no time for you to hide and never
stand and stare,
but you know you can't escape us,
now that you're totally bare.

Dean Landau (11)
Woodside Park International School, Barnet

SNOW AND ICE

So sharp,
So cold,
So clear,
Falling soft and crisp,

So white,
So deadly,
So glistening,
Blows a gentle kiss,

A white blanket covers the ground
Like it's tucking it in for the night,

It's sharp, cold and menacing
Watch out for its deadly bite.

Frances Luiz (11)
Woodside Park International School, Barnet

DARKNESS

Night came and never left
Her world forever shadowed
She wished that her dark night
Would sometime soon unravel
For now she bears a stick
Wherever she can travel

Click went the stick as she wandered down the road
Click went the stick as she carried her heavy load
Click went the stick as she wobbled down the lane
Click went the stick as she stumbled in the rain

Struggling to live life
As normal as can be
Trying to make peace
With those she could not see
Fighting to survive
In the darkness of the world
Hoping that one day
Her story would be told.

David Phillips (11)
Woodside Park International School, Barnet

AUTUMN

Red, yellow, brown
leaves fall down.
They are singing and dancing
sideways and backwards
and dye themselves to colours.
They dance their best dance
to see who is the best.

Rena Isomura (12)
Woodside Park International School, Barnet

THE MOTHER OF GIRLS

Skirt is lying on the dinner table
Shoes with an expensive designer label
Their room shows signs of wear
There is make-up scattered here and there.

Pictures of their boyfriends on the wall
The ones who fail to call
There are trousers hanging on the bed
Their room is so messy it spins my head!
I spend the morning combing the curls
How did you guess I am the mother of girls!

Sive Ozer (11)
Woodside Park International School, Barnet

A WALK IN THE COUNTRYSIDE

Sprinting along a winding path,
Then suddenly it splits in half.
I pick which path to go along
Hoping it is the right one, not wrong.
I look around to see what I can see
And then I stumble across a 100-year-old oak tree.
I clamber up and look around to see what lies around me,
I see a small river trickling by slowly,
An abandoned cave looking lonely,
A bumblebee buzzing away there,
A cute baby hare walking elsewhere,
From hidden corners that you don't expect
Beautiful blooms and many an insect,
Wild cats running ever so fast like lightning,
Looking ever so frightening.
I was truly amazed at what I saw,
But then came an amazing thing, a wild boar!
I run out of the countryside shrieking, 'Someone please help.'
All I do on my way home is yelp.
I run into my house, into my room and jump on my bed
And then I think about all of the things that are still in my head.

Netta Lander (11)
Woodside Park International School, Barnet

ON THE FARM

As the pigs come for their midday meal,
In fly the birds and begin to steal.
While the white hen catches the worm,
Blackie the horse just stands quite firm.
Come little ducklings, swim with me!
All together now, one, two, three.
In the spring young lambs are gay
And Mother watches as they play.

Sofia Samrad (11)
Woodside Park International School, Barnet

COMICS

Comics are the best to read
Something to satisfy my need
So they are the best
But they won't get you through a test

They have very funny clips
When there are I have some sips
I read them every day
Even when I play

It is something to never put down
It doesn't even make you frown
It is interesting in a special way
That I never put them in a pile of hay.

Purav Desai (11)
Woodside Park International School, Barnet